The Golden Age of the Poster

SELECTED AND EDITED BY

HAYWARD AND BLANCHE CIRKER

DOVER PUBLICATIONS, INC., NEW YORK

Published in Canada by General Publishing Company, Ltd., 30 Lesmill Road, Don Mills, Toronto, Ontario.
Published in the United Kingdom by Constable and Company, Ltd., 10 Orange Street, London WC 2.

The Golden Age of the Poster is a new work first published by Dover Publications, Inc., in 1971. The sources of the illustrations are given in the Note below.

International Standard Book Number: 0-486-22753-7
Library of Congress Catalog Card Number: 79-164736

Manufactured in the United States of America
Dover Publications, Inc.
180 Varick Street
New York, N.Y. 10014

NOTE ON SOURCES

Plates 4, 5, 40, 44, 54, 59 and 70 are reproduced from the book *Les Affiches Étrangères illustrées* (separate sections written by M. Bauwens, T. Hayashi, La Forgue, J. Meier-Graefe and J. Pennell), published by G. Boudet, Paris, 1897, in a limited edition of 1050 copies.

All the rest are reproduced from single-sheet facsimiles in the series *Les Maîtres de l'Affiche,* which was published monthly by the Imprimerie Chaix, Paris, from December 1895 through November 1900 at the rate of four numbered facsimiles per month (excluding occasional unnumbered bonus sheets)—thus totaling 240 facsimiles in 60 monthly issues. The List of Illustrations in the present volume gives the original facsimile number, issue number, month and year of every item reproduced from *Les Maîtres de l'Affiche.*

The arrangement of plates in this volume (except for the Frontispiece) is strictly alphabetical by the names of the artists. Biographical data on the artists will be found following the Plates.

Plate 70, Walker's poster for *The Woman in White,* is exceptional here in two ways—it is earlier than the rest (1871) and it is a work in black and white—but because of its fame, merit and pioneering importance, it could not be omitted from a representative collection of golden age posters.

List of Illustrations

The entries in this list give the following information (where available and where applicable) in the following order:

Artist's name (nationality in parentheses): product, firm or event advertised in poster (in parentheses: city where original poster was printed, original printer, original date); dimensions of original poster in inches, height before width, based throughout on the metric dimensions given in *Les Maîtres de l'Affiche;* (finally, in parentheses, the original plate number in *Les Maîtres de l'Affiche,* abbreviated M.A., as well as the original *Maîtres* issue number and date).

2　Anonymous　(Czech)

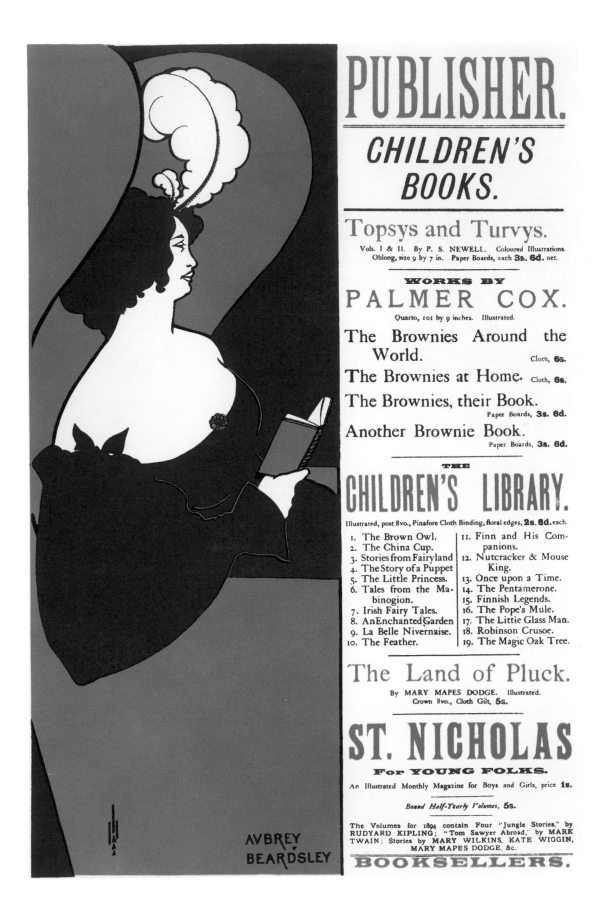

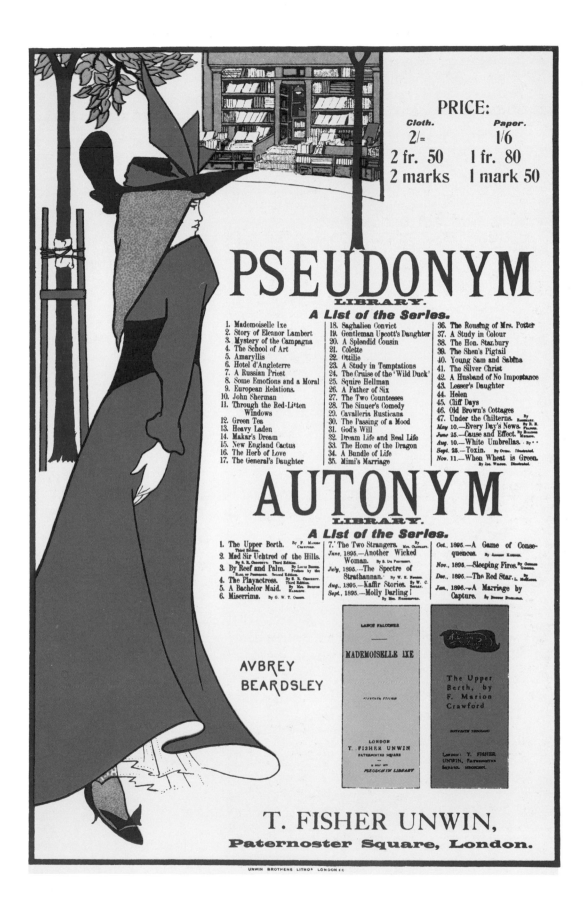

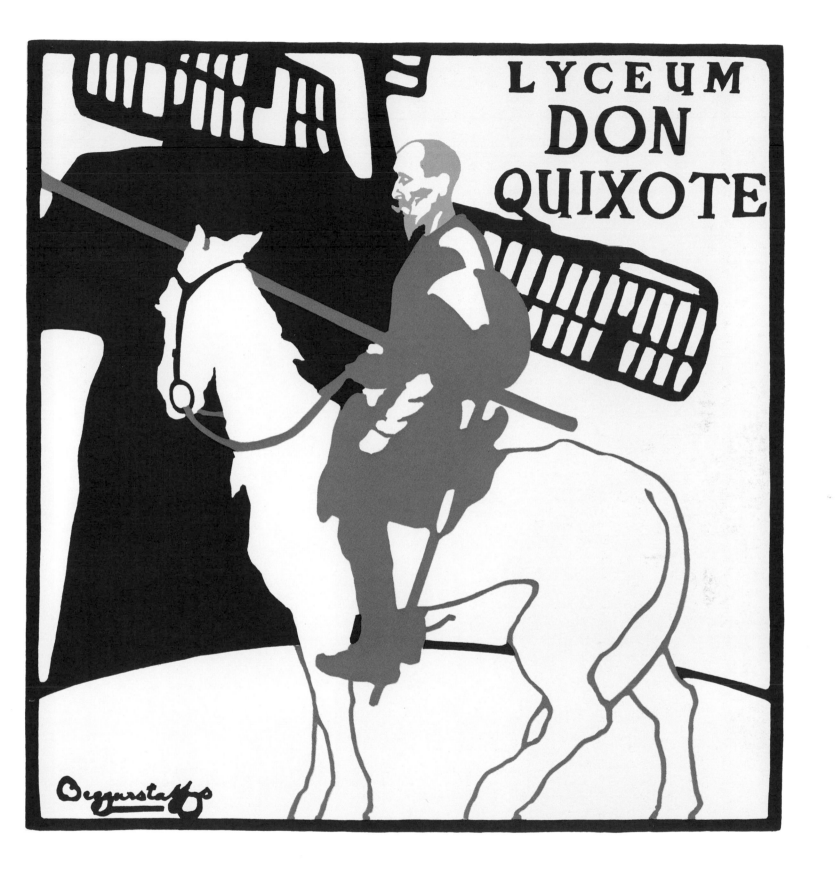

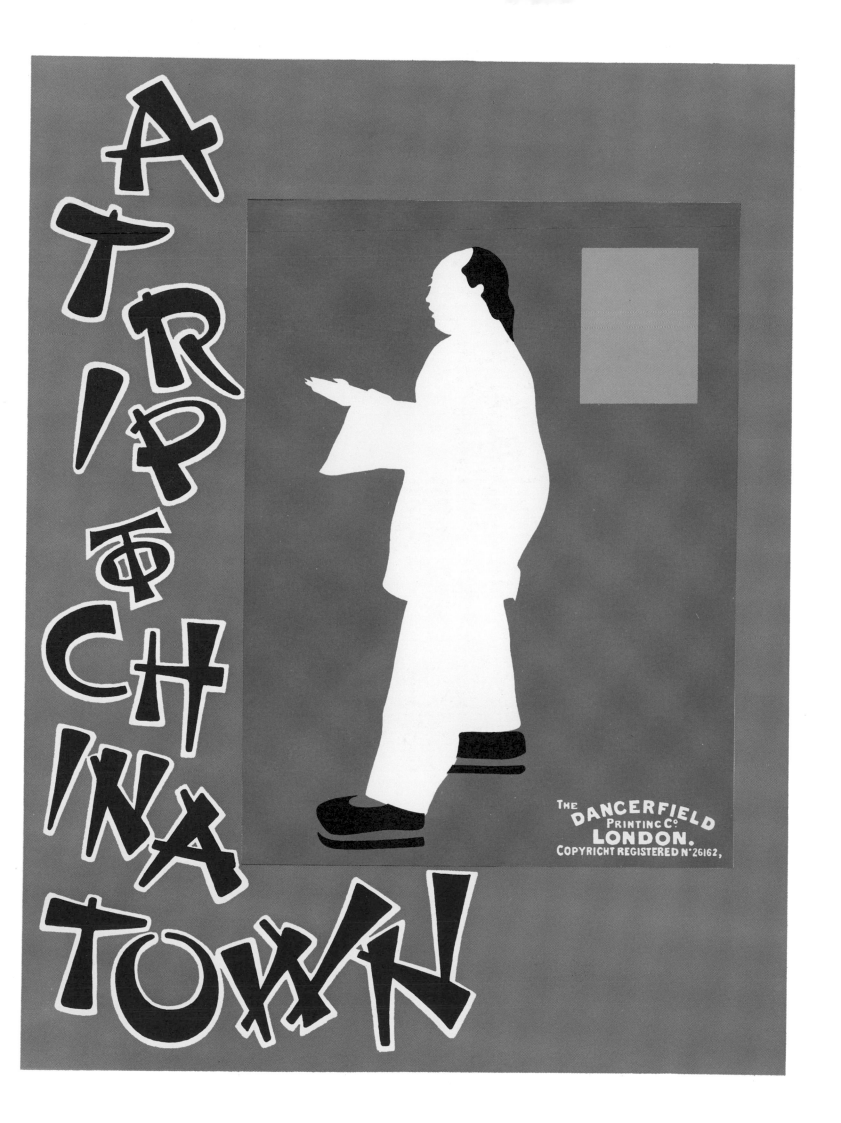

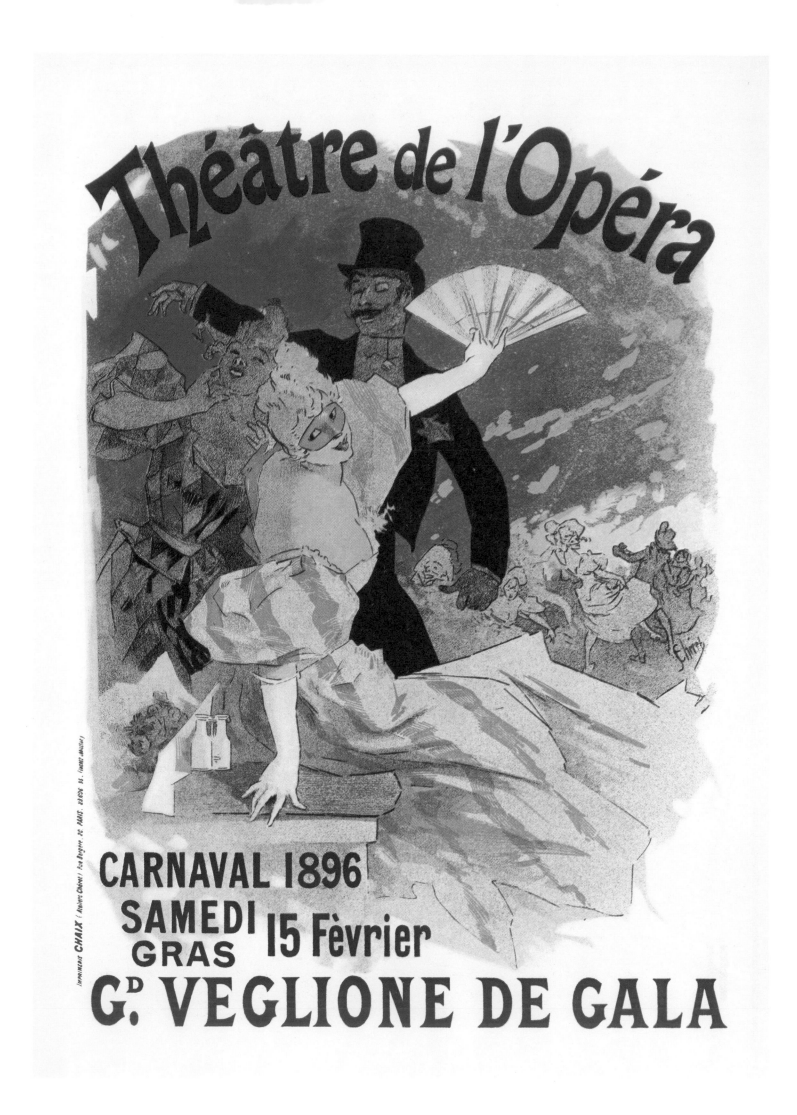

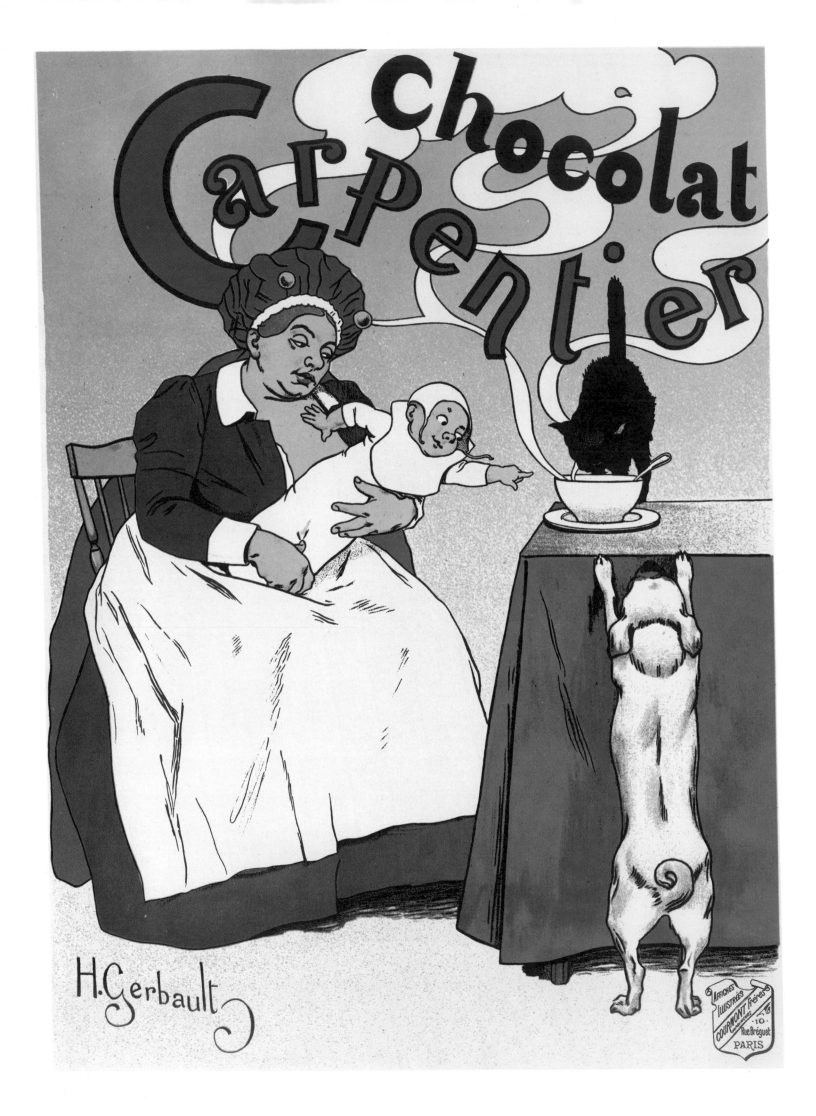

2ᵉ EXPOSITION DES PEINTRES LITHOGRAPHES

DU 10 au 25 Janvier

SALLE DU FIGARO RUE DROUOT

ATELIER, GOTTLOB 45. Rue de Belleville.

IMP.ᴵᴱˢ LEMERCIER, PARIS.

Fernand-Louis Gottlob 29

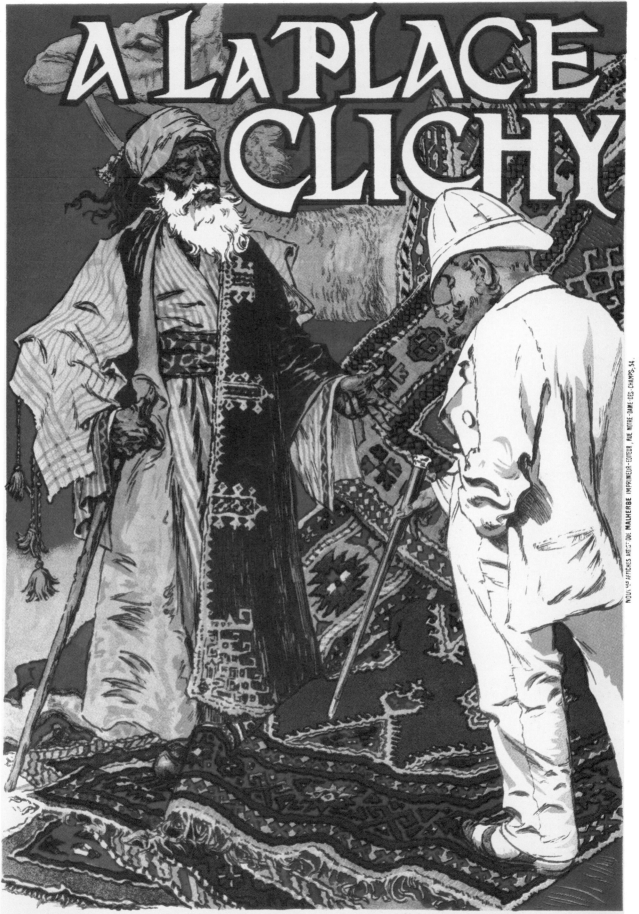

THE CHIEFTAIN

BY
F. C BURNAND
&
ARTHUR
SULLIVAN

Dudley Hardy

SAVOY THEATRE.

WATERLOW & SONS.LTD.LITH.LONDON WALL.LONDON E.C.

COPYRIGHT REGD

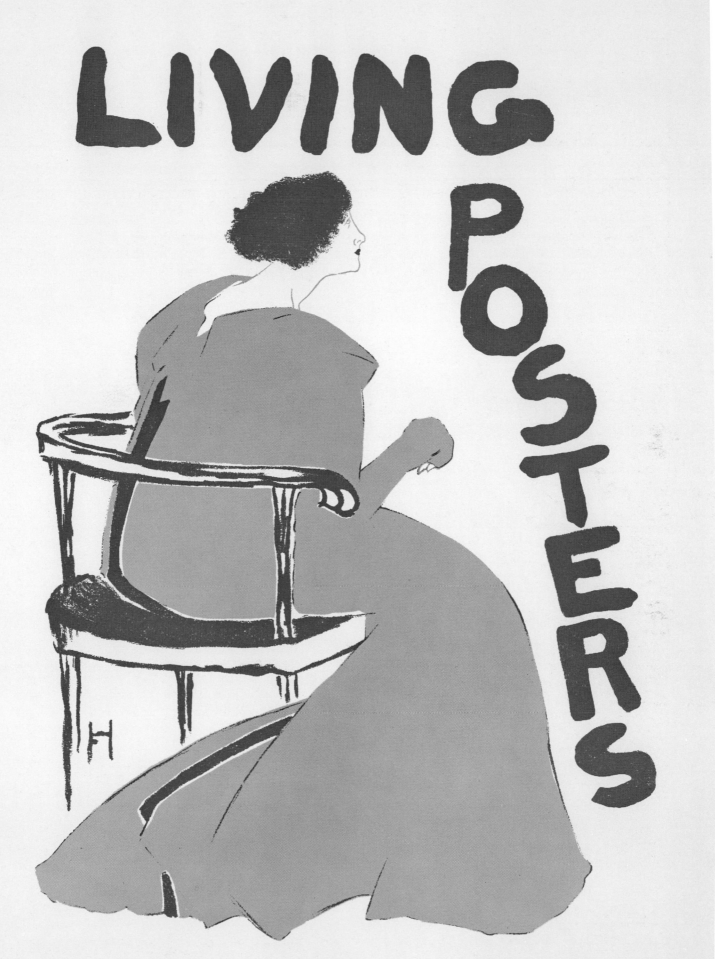

Designed By Frank Hazenplug: Printed By Stone & Kimball, Chicago

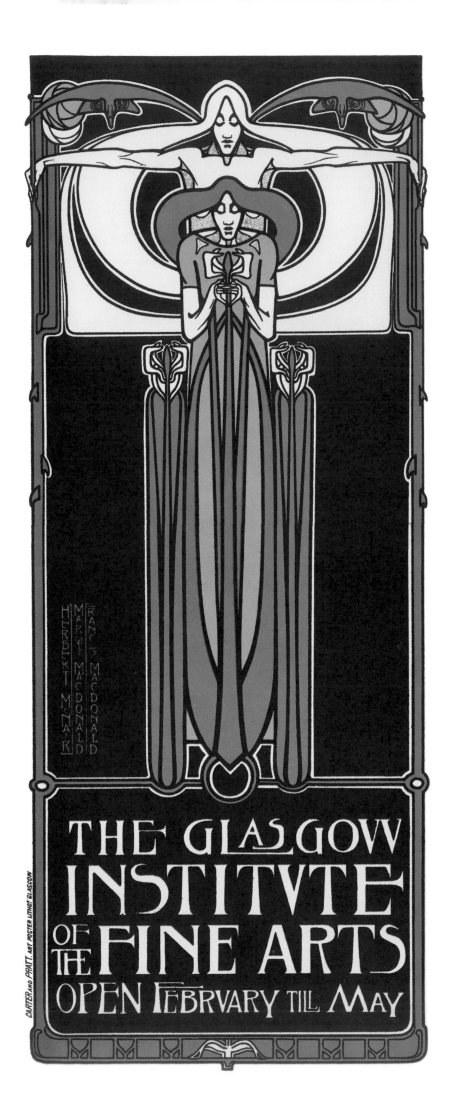

44   Herbert McNair, Margaret Macdonald, Frances Macdonald

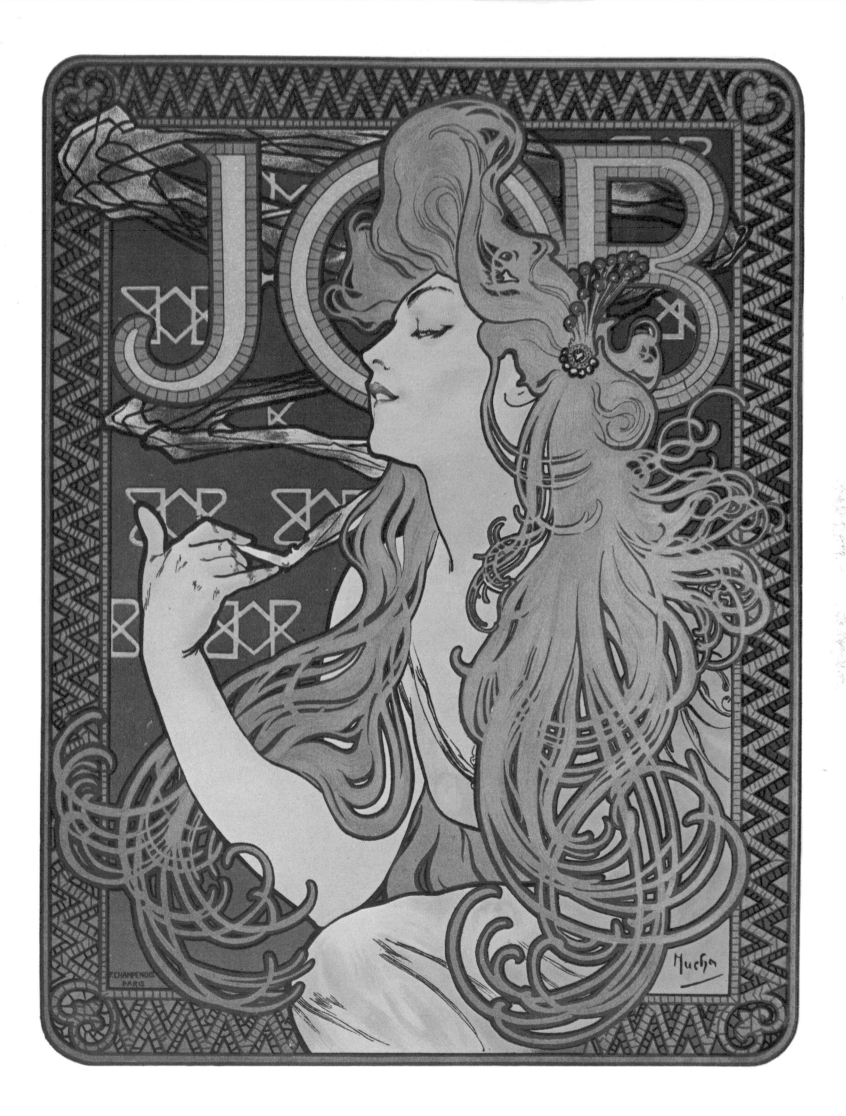

THE CENTURY

Midsummer.
Holiday Number.
August.

SECOND PRIZE CENTURY POSTER CONTEST.
[COPYRIGHT 1897 BY THE CENTURY CO]

ELIHU VEDDER
F. HOPKINSON SMITH   } JUDGES
HENRY J. HARDENBERGH

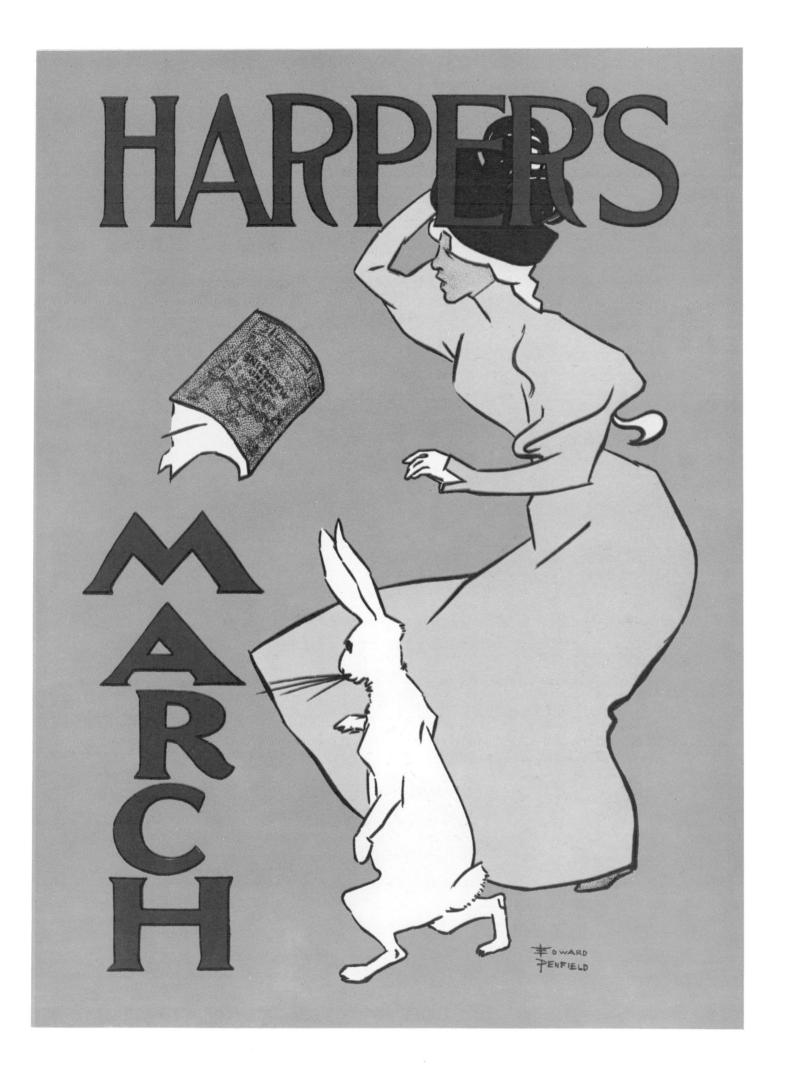

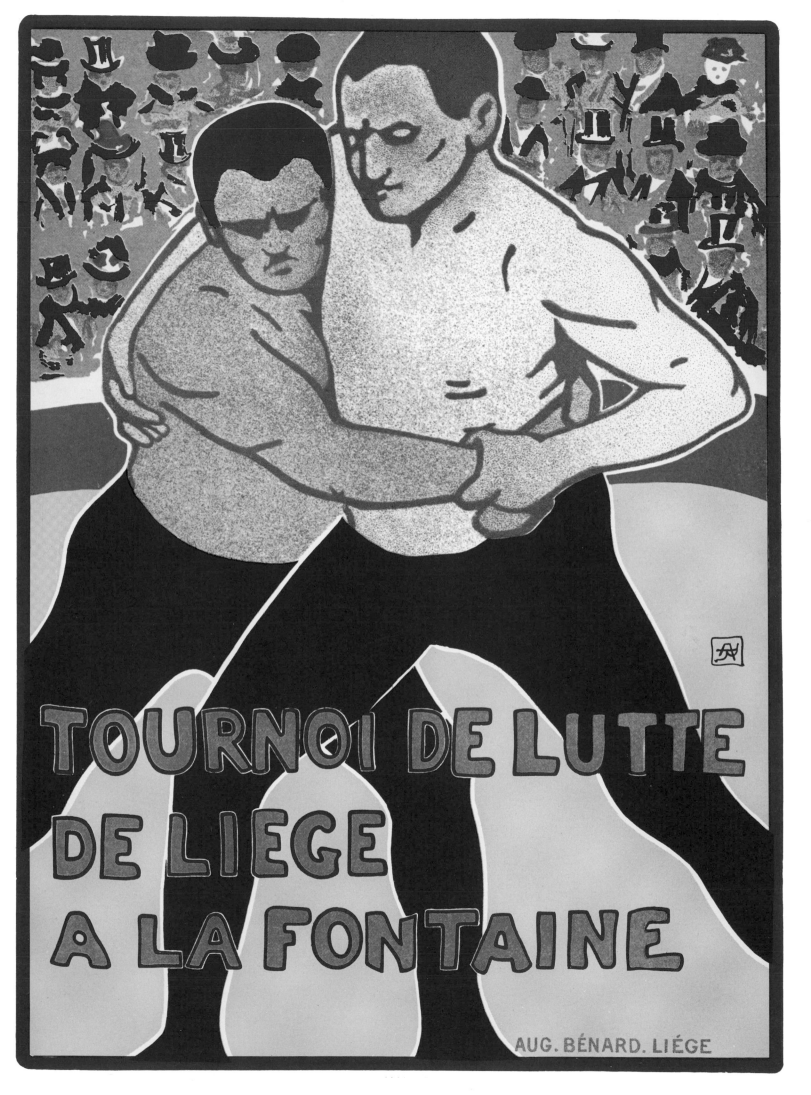

Lait pur de la Vingeanne Stérilisé

Imp CHARLES VERNEAU 114 Rue Oberkampf. PARIS. (DÉPOSÉ)

Steinlen

Quillot frères
Montigny sur Vingeanne
Côte d'Or

La revue blanche

bi-mensuelle

le n° 60 cent.

12 francs par An

1 rue Laffitte

Paris

Charpentier et Fasquelle, éditeurs
11, rue de Grenelle

AH!
LA PÉ...LA PÉ...
LA PÉPINIÈRE !!!
REVUE
en deux actes et quatre tableaux de M.M.
ALBERT PAJOL et ADOLPHE COUTURET
AIRS NOUVEAUX MUSIQUE ARRANGÉE et BALLET de M. JACOUTOT
Costumes dessinés par JAPHET exécutés par Mme Louise CAFFARD, décors de M. MÉNESSIER
DISTRIBUTION

M. Mmes DAMOYE, la Pépinière—MELRY la Mère Python, la Brigadière,1ère Coltineuse, la France—DELLY-MÔ, l'Omnibus nocturne,3ème Agent, Un Poney, le sou italien la Russie—JAMES, Marchande de poissons, l'Ouvreuse, DEBAY, la Buvette, 2me Agent, Un Poney, le Chat Anglais, Madame Satan—EMILIENNE Une Artiste, Un Python, Un Poney, la Présentatrice—TERVILLE, le Ridicule,1er Agent, Un Poney, le Baiser—KERSIN, l'Habit noir, Un Jockey, l'Affiche Artistique MONTIGNY, Un Télégraphiste 4me Agent, 2me Coltineuse, la Perruche, le Chat du Diable—CARBET, l'Avre, l'habit jaune, Un Jockey, la Demoiselle des Postes—SAINT- LOT, la Folliculaire, l'Habit vert, Un Jockey, la Valkyrie, la Paix—MARTHELETTY, Un Python, la Parisienne DALIGNY, Un Python, l'Habit rouge, Un Jockey, l'Orthographe,

M. Mrs RANSARD, le Boulevard—HELT, le Régisseur, l'Envouteur—2me Médecin, le Dompteur—DUREL Un Monsieur Un Cocher 5me Médecin, Un Candidat, 1er Napoléon—MAX-HIM, le Soleil, l'Ambulancier, 3me Médecin, Un Candidat, le Beau bat-d'l'air ALBENS le Paysan Un Soldat, Un Malade, Sarah-RENNEVAL, le Chef d'Orchestre, Paris, 2me Médecin—FERNANDEZ, Un Machiniste Un Vitrien Un Marin Belge, Un Gardien l'Academicien Un Candidat, Deuxième Napoléon, DESFORGES— Un Pompier, Un Détenu, 4e Médecin, Un Candidat, Un Ours—LUCIEN, Un Marchand d'habits Un Soldat, Un Afficheur, Un Ours,

TOUS les SOIRS à 9½ h. DIMANCHES et FÊTES MATINÉES à 2 HEURES
CONCERT de la PÉPINIÈRE (près la gare St Lazare.)

PAJOL & Cie EDITEURS 27, Rue Bergère.

Félix-Édouard Vallotton   69

The Artists

LOUIS ANQUETIN (French; 1861–1932): pupil of Manet; independent, influenced by Degas and Van Gogh; painted portraits, figures, scenes; designed tapestry cartoons; produced a few lithographs.

AUBREY VINCENT BEARDSLEY (English; 1872–1898): self-taught, precocious genius of draftsmanship; an eclectic original enamored of Renaissance art; exemplified fin-de-siècle sensuality and neurasthenia; drawings for *Morte Darthur, Salome, Rape of the Lock;* frequent contributor to *Yellow Book;* did many book covers and several posters for publishers and theaters.

THE BEGGARSTAFFS: Under this double pseudonym, Nicholson and Pryde created the modern woodcut poster, with clear outlines and large expanses of flat color.
    SIR WILLIAM NICHOLSON (English; 1872–1949): renewer of the English woodcut tradition; painter, especially of portraits; costume designer.
    JAMES PRYDE (Scottish; 1866–1941): painter and wood engraver.

ÉMILE BERCHMANS (Belgian; born 1867): painter, pastelist, etcher, lithographer; did drawings for books and magazines and various strong posters.

PAUL BERTHON (French; active in Paris around 1900): illustrator and poster artist influenced by style of Grasset.

PIERRE BONNARD (French; 1867–1947): major painter and graphic artist; his posters date from his early, decorative period; graphic style influenced by Toulouse-Lautrec; did many book illustrations; in painting, began as one of the "Nabis," later gave a new interpretation to Impressionism, employing an unusual range of bold colors.

MAURICE BOUTET DE MONVEL (French; 1851–1913): painter (including religious and Oriental scenes), watercolorist, illustrator of many books, especially juveniles.

WILL BRADLEY (American; 1868–1962): "dean of American designers and art editors"; prolific designer of covers, posters, book illustrations influenced by Beardsley; founder of Wayside Press; did *Chap-Books* for American Type Founders; art director of *Collier's, Good Housekeeping,* etc.; writer; type designer; stage and movie designer.

CARAN D'ACHE (French; 1858 or 1859–1909): pseudonym of Emmanuel Poiré, renowned caricaturist and illustrator, influenced by Busch and Oberländer; born in Moscow, used Russian word for pencil (*karandásh*) as *nom de plume;* excelled in military subjects; contributor to *Le Figaro, La Caricature,* etc.; creator of puppets and cabaret puppet shows.

WILLIAM CARQUEVILLE (American; born 1871): chiefly known for his posters for *Lippincott's.*

F.-A. CAZALS (French; 1865–1941): magazine and book illustrator; wrote poems and songs; famous chiefly for his lithographic portraits of his friend Verlaine.

JULES CHÉRET (French; 1836–1932): leading lithographer; set up his own shop, specializing in posters, in 1866 (in 1881 this shop became the Imprimerie Chaix, publishers of *Les Maîtres de l'Affiche*); after selling shop, continued doing commercial graphics, but also paintings, tapestry cartoons, etc.; combining rococo grace and modern Parisian elegance, created a true poster style (rather than imitation of oil paintings); first major poster artist to draw directly on lithographic stone.

ADOLPHE-LOUIS-CHARLES CRESPIN (Belgian; born 1859): art nouveau painter; decorated walls of Belgian churches and public buildings; teacher at Belgian Royal Academy; important poster artist from 1887 on.

HENRI-JACQUES-ÉDOUARD EVENEPOEL (Belgian; 1872–1899): pupil of Crespin in Belgium, of Gustave Moreau in Paris; painter and graphic artist with strong sense of color; specialized in depiction of children.

GEORGES DE FEURE (French; 1868–1928): pupil of Chéret; did many posters; painter, lithographer, engraver, illustrator; designer of theater decorations, porcelains, furniture and furnishings (in the style of van de Velde).

OTTO FISCHER (German; 1870–1947): painter, etcher, lithographer, designer of applied art; around 1895, helped to create the modern German artistic poster; did chiefly graphics up to 1906, later did various oils.

HENRI GERBAULT (French; 1863–1930): did humorous illustrations for magazines and books; also watercolorist.

FERNAND-LOUIS GOTTLOB (French; born 1873): lithographer, illustrator, portrait painter.

EUGÈNE-SAMUEL GRASSET (French; 1841–1917): born in Switzerland, became French citizen in 1891; sculptor, illustrator (influenced by Doré), designer of applied art (influenced by Viollet-le-Duc), poster artist, painter, architect; stained-glass style in evidence in the poster for his own show.

MAURICE GREIFFENHAGEN (English; 1862–1921): figure and portrait painter influenced by Renaissance art and Pre-Raphaelites; did much illustration from 1887 on (magazines, novels by Rider Haggard); the *Pall Mall Budget* poster was epoch-making.

JULES-ALEXANDRE GRÜN (French; 1868–1934): painter, pastelist, magazine illustrator, cabaret decorator; poster style influenced by Vallotton; bold use of black-and-white or two-color work (red as second color).

ALBERT GUILLAUME (French; 1873–1942): humorous illustrations for magazines and books; paintings (studied with Gérôme); posters influenced by Chéret; facile and "modern."

DUDLEY HARDY (English; 1866–1922): painter (several works of social import), magazine illustrator, designer of posters and magazine advertisements.

FRANK HAZENPLUG (American; born 1873): Chicago illustrator (*Chap-Book*) and poster artist.

THOMAS THEODOR HEINE (German; 1867–1948): painter,

illustrator, poster artist, designer of applied art; contributor to magazines *Jugend* and *Fliegende Blätter;* in 1896, cofounder of *Simplicissimus* (famous for championing social justice), stayed with that magazine to 1933; after 1933, lived outside of Germany, finally settled in Sweden.

ADOLF HOHENSTEIN (German; born 1854): born in St. Petersburg, worked in Italy and Germany; painted, did posters for Ricordi in Milan (including the one for Puccini's *La Bohème*).

FRED HYLAND (English): no information available.

HENRI-GABRIEL IBELS (French; 1867–1936?): painter, graphic artist, book illustrator, poster artist; did political cartoons concerning the Dreyfus affair; friend of Toulouse-Lautrec, who began lithography at Ibels' insistence.

MARGARET MACDONALD, FRANCES MACDONALD (Scottish): sisters, taught in Glasgow; Margaret married the eminent artist and architect Charles Rennie Mackintosh.

HERBERT McNAIR (Scottish): no information available.

HENRI-GEORGES-JEAN-ISIDORE MEUNIER (Belgian; 1873–1922): painter, etcher, lithographer; nephew of the great sculptor Constantin Meunier.

ALBERT GEORGE MORROW (English; 1863–1927): painter, illustrator, poster artist.

ALFONS (ALPHONSE) MARIA MUCHA (Czech; 1860–1939): one of the main exponents of art nouveau (chief work done in France); painter; graphic artist; designer of stained-glass windows, furniture, carpets, stage sets; important book illustrator and calendar artist; major figure in poster history, his first Bernhardt poster (the one for *Gismonda*, 1894) winning him lasting fame.

MAXFIELD PARRISH (American; 1870–1966): pupil of Howard Pyle; book and magazine illustrator; painter of figures and landscapes.

EDWARD PENFIELD (American; 1866–1925): painter, illustrator, lithographer; art director of *Harper's, Harper's Weekly* and *Harper's Bazaar* from 1891 to 1901; has been called the originator of the poster in America; designed all *Harper's* posters from 1893 to 1899.

ARMAND RASSENFOSSE (Belgian; 1862–1934): etcher, painter, book illustrator, poster artist, bookplate designer; started as businessman, became artist at about thirty, with the encouragement and instruction of Félicien Rops; great experimenter in graphic media, inventor of a color engraving technique.

ETHEL REED (American; born 1876): painter and illustrator.

FRITZ REHM (German; born 1871): illustrator, designed posters and bookplates.

W(ALFORD) GRAHAM ROBERTSON (English; 1866–1948): painter of portraits and landscapes, book illustrator, costume designer; poet, author of numerous books and plays.

JOSEF SATTLER (German; 1867–1931): prolific illustrator and etcher; did many drawings and watercolors; worked for magazine *Pan* from 1895 to 1897.

THÉOPHILE-ALEXANDRE STEINLEN (Swiss/French; 1859–1923): great chronicler of Montmartre life; etcher, painter, lithographer; born in Switzerland, to Paris 1882, French citizen 1901; contributed to many magazines; did book illustrations; decorated café walls.

M. LOUISE STOWELL (American; still active around 1930): born and worked in Rochester, N.Y.; pupil of Arthur W. Dow; specialized in watercolors.

HENRI-MARIE-RAYMOND DE TOULOUSE-LAUTREC-MONFA (French; 1864–1901): indefatigable sketcher of Parisian night life and lowlife; influenced by Degas and Japanese art; painter and (from about 1893, prodded by Ibels) lithographer; exerted widespread influence (especially on the young Picasso); his world-famous posters, menus and invitations were printed in very small quantities, and originals have long been exceedingly rare.

FÉLIX-ÉDOUARD VALLOTTON (French-Swiss; 1865–1925): painter and graphic artist, aiming at strength and clarity of form; has been called "the Swiss Ingres"; in Paris from 1882; book and magazine illustrator; one of the renewers of the art of the woodcut.

FRED(ERICK) WALKER (English; 1840–1875): painter, woodcut designer, book and magazine illustrator; called "the Tennyson of painting"; influenced by Pre-Raphaelites; his poster for *The Woman in White* was one of the first English artistic posters.